Fingerpow

T0039439

Level Six

Effective Technic for All Piano Methods
by John W. Schaum

Foreword

Strong fingers are an important requirement for all pianists, amateur and professional. Schaum Fingerpower® exercises are designed to strengthen all five fingers of both hands. Equal hand development is assured through the performance of the same patterns in each hand, either in parallel motion or with alternating hands.

The exercises are purposely short and easily memorized. This enables the student to focus his/her efforts on the technical benefits, attentive listening and to playing with a steady beat.

To derive the full benefit of these exercises, careful attention must be given to how they are practiced. They should be played with a firm, solid finger action. The student must listen carefully during practice. It is important to be aware of the feeling in the fingers and hands while playing. The student should try to play each finger equally loud. Each hand should also be equally loud.

The exercises are progressive, becoming gradually more challenging as the student goes through each level. The exercises are brief and condensed, so they will easily fit in with a student's other musical assignments. There are opportunities for phrase development, rhythmic variety and different types of touch.

The Fingerpower® series consists of seven books, Primer Level through Level 6. The Primer Level may be started by a beginner after only six to eight weeks of study.

The first five Fingerpower® books (Primer through Level 4) have accompaniment CDs and MIDI diskettes available. The accompaniments provide an incentive for accurate playing, while making practice more enjoyable. The MIDI diskettes have the versatility of separate tracks for right hand, left hand, harmony, bass and rhythm as well as adjustable tempo.

Schaum Publications, Inc.
10235 N. Port Washington Rd. • Mequon, WI 53092 • www.schaumpiano.net

ISBN-13: 978-1-936098-07-1

Exclusively Distributed By

HAL•LEONARD®
CORPORATION
7777 W. BLUEMOUND RD. P.O. BOX 13819 MILWAUKEE, WI 53213

Contents

1. Melodic and Broken Chord Patterns

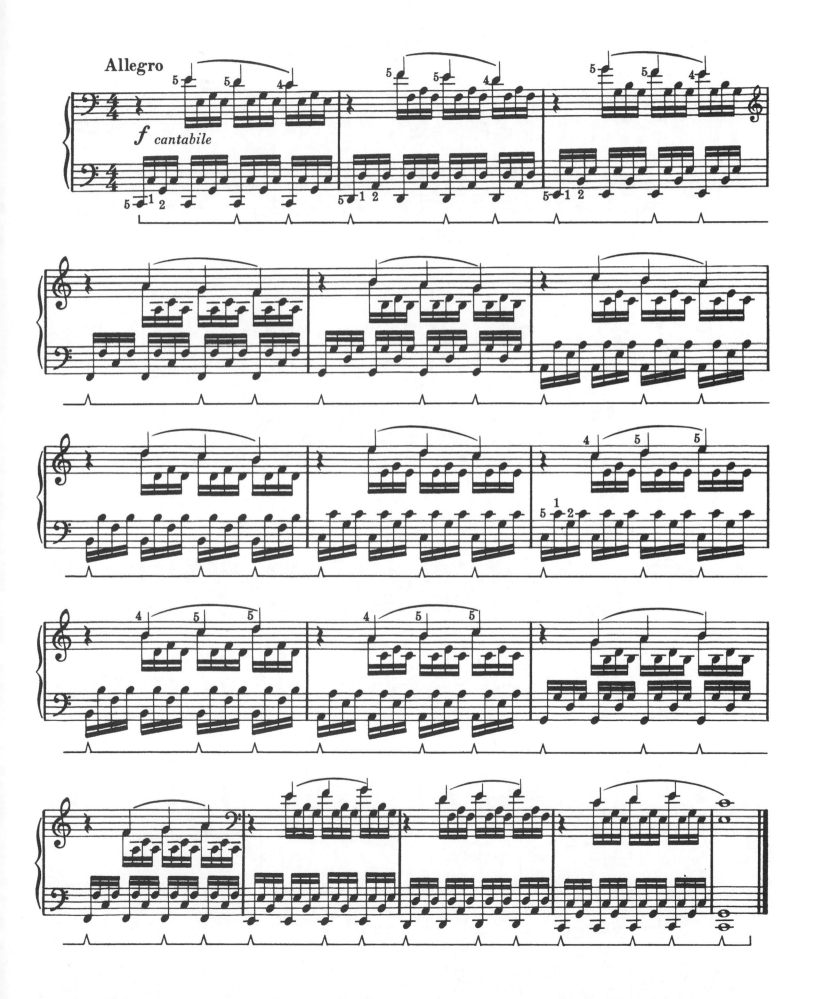

2. Chromatic Broken Chord Inversions

Note: A finger number in parenthesis is an alternate.

3. Major Scales of C, G, D, and A
(Two Octaves - Hands Together)

C Major

G Major

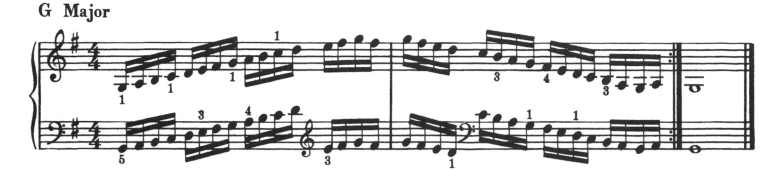

D Major

A Major

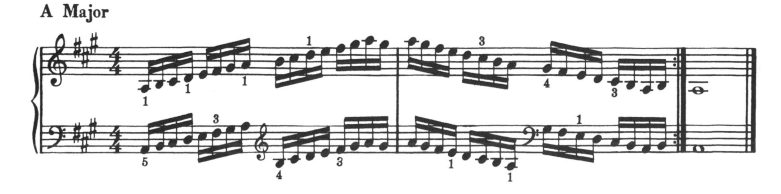

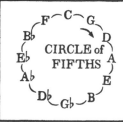

CIRCLE of FIFTHS

In vocal scand instrumental music, the harmony frequently progresses Tin the order of the CIRCLE of FIFTHS. Consequently, in the John W. Schaum FINGERPOWER Book 6, the scales are presented in this succession.

4. Major Scales of E, B, G♭, and D♭
(Two Octaves - Hands Together)

E Major

B Major (Enharmonic with C♭ major - See chart below)

G♭ Major (Enharmonic with F♯ major - See chart below)

D♭ Major (Enharmonic with C♯ major - See chart below)

ENHARMONIC MAJOR SCALE CHART

The major scales of C♭, F♯ and C♯ have the same sound and keyboard formation as the major scales of B, G♭ and D♭. Consequently they are ENHARMONICALLY the same.

C♭ Major
Seven Flats: B♭,E♭,A♭,D♭,G♭,C♭,F♭

Enharmonic with B major

F♯ Major
Six Sharps: F♯,C♯,G♯,D♯,A♯,E♯

Enharmonic with G♭ major

C♯ Major
Seven Sharps: F♯,C♯,G♯,D♯,A♯,E♯,B♯

Enharmonic with D♭ major

5. Major Scales of A♭, E♭, B♭, and F
(Two Octaves - Hands Together)

A♭ Major

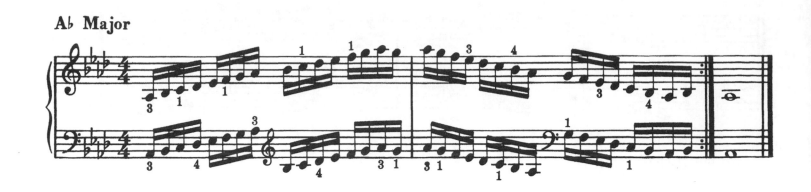

E♭ Major

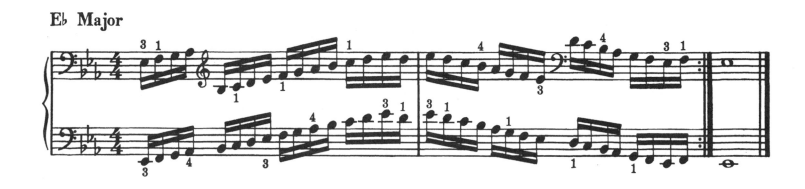

B♭ Major

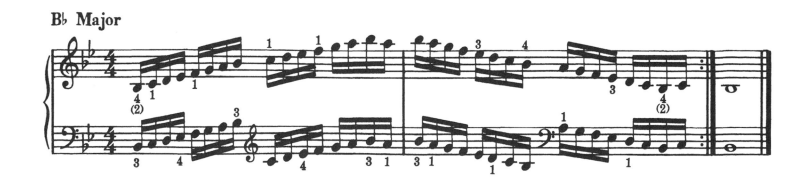

F Major

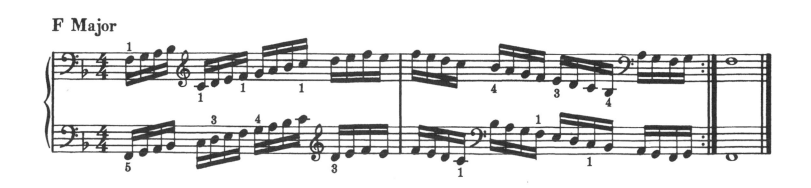

6. Major Arpeggios of C, G, D , and A
(Four Octaves - Hands Together)

C Major

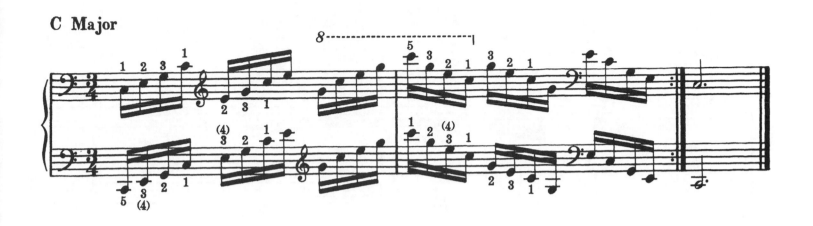

G Major

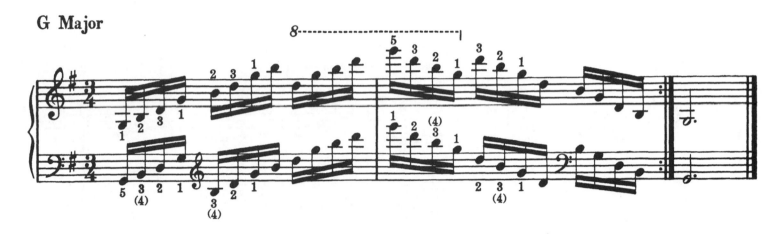

D Major

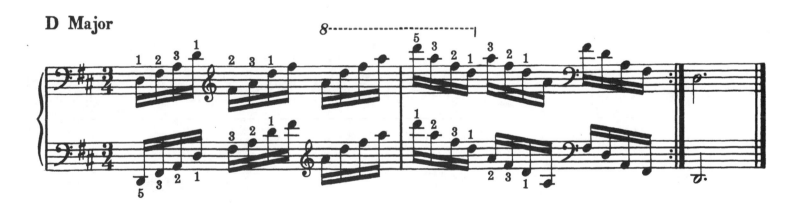

A Major

7. Major Arpeggios of E, B, G♭, and D♭
(Four Octaves - Hands Together)

E Major

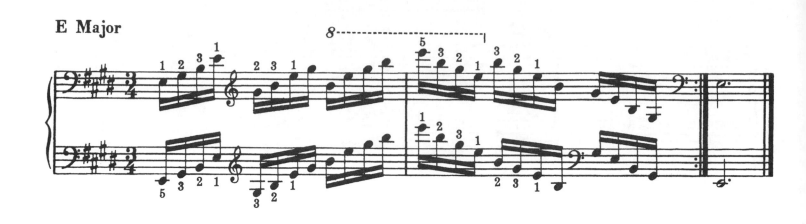

B Major

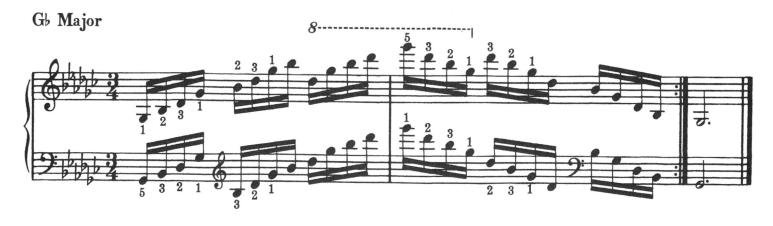

G♭ Major

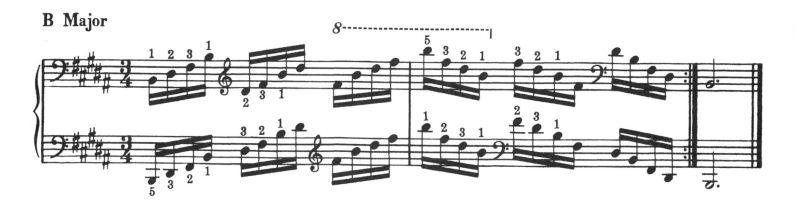

D♭ Major

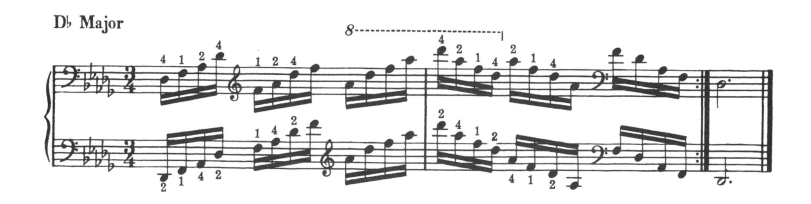

8. Major Arpeggios of A♭, E♭, B♭, and F
(Four Octaves - Hands Together)

A♭ Major

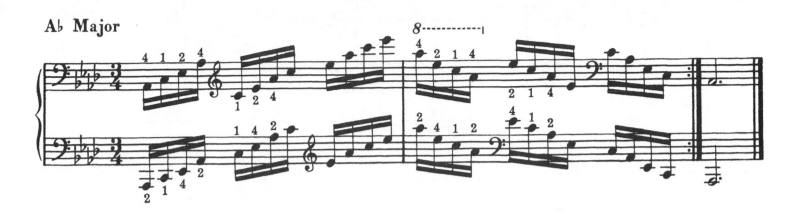

E♭ Major

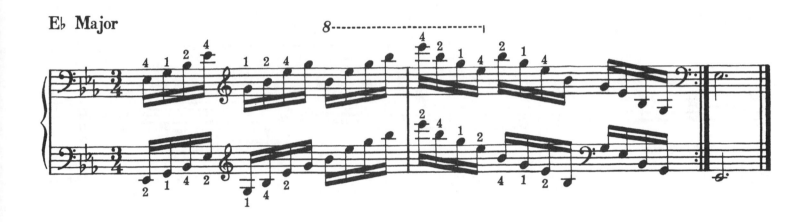

B♭ Major

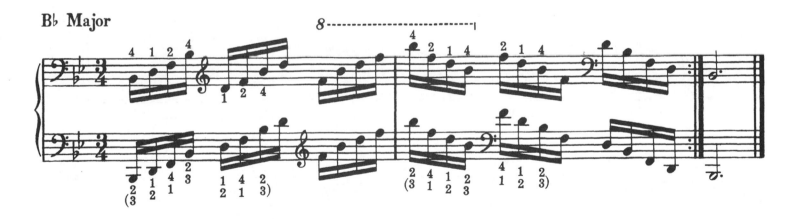

F Major

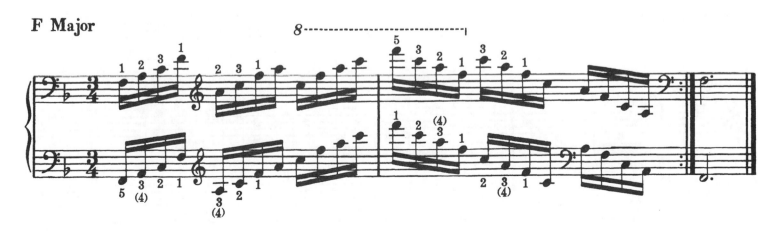

9. Major Preludes in All Keys

10. Melody and Accompaniment in Same Hand

Moderato

11. Augmented Arpeggios of C, G, D, and A
(Four Octaves - Hands Together)

NOTE: Actually there are only four augmented arpeggios. Study the chart below, and notice how the twelve augmented triads of the CIRCLE OF FIFTHS are reduced to the four basic triads at the top of each of the following columns.

C				G				D				A			
	C	E	G#		G	B	D#		D	F#	A#		A	C#	E#
	E	G#	B#		B	D#	F×		Gb	Bb	D		Db	F	A
	Ab	C	E		Eb	G	B		Bb	D	F#		F	A	C#

12. Harmonic Minor Scales of A, E, B, and F#
(Two Octaves - Hands Together)

All minor scales start on the sixth tone of the relative major. All minor key signatures are the same as the relative major. The rule for the HARMONIC minor scale is to raise the seventh degree a half step ascending and descending.

A Harmonic Minor (Relative to C Major)

E Harmonic Minor (Relative to G Major)

B Harmonic Minor (Relative to D Major)

F# Harmonic Minor (Relative to A Major)

The NATURAL and MELODIC minors are presented below for analytical purposes. They may also be performed two octaves - hands together. (Optional)

The NATURAL minor scale follows the exact signature of the relative major without any alteration. The NATURAL minor is also known as the PURE or NORMAL minor.

The MELODIC minor scale consists of raising the 6th and 7th degrees ascending but restoring them to NATURAL minor form when descending.

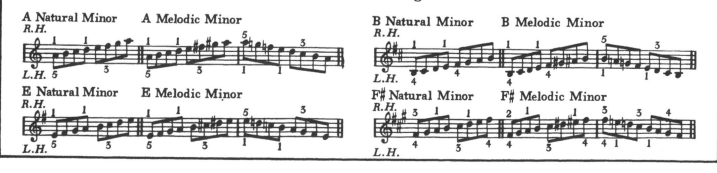

13. Harmonic Minor Scales of C#, G#, Eb, and Bb
(Two Octaves - Hands Together)

C# Harmonic Minor (Relative to E Major)

G# Harmonic Minor (Relative to B Major)

Eb Harmonic Minor (Relative to Gb Major)

Bb Harmonic Minor (Relative to Db Major)

C# Natural Minor   C# Melodic Minor

Eb Natural Minor   Eb Melodic Minor

G# Natural Minor   G# Melodic Minor

Bb Natural Minor   Bb Melodic Minor

18

14. Harmonic Minor Scales of F, C, G, and D
(Two Octaves - Hands Together)

F Harmonic Minor (Relative to A♭ Major)

C Harmonic Minor (Relative to E♭ Major)

G Harmonic Minor (Relative to B♭ Major)

D Harmonic Minor (Relative to F Major)

F Natural Minor   F Melodic Minor

G Natural Minor   G Melodic Minor

C Natural Minor   C Melodic Minor

D Natural Minor   D Melodic Minor

15. Minor Arpeggios of A, E, B, and F#
(Four Octaves - Hands Together)

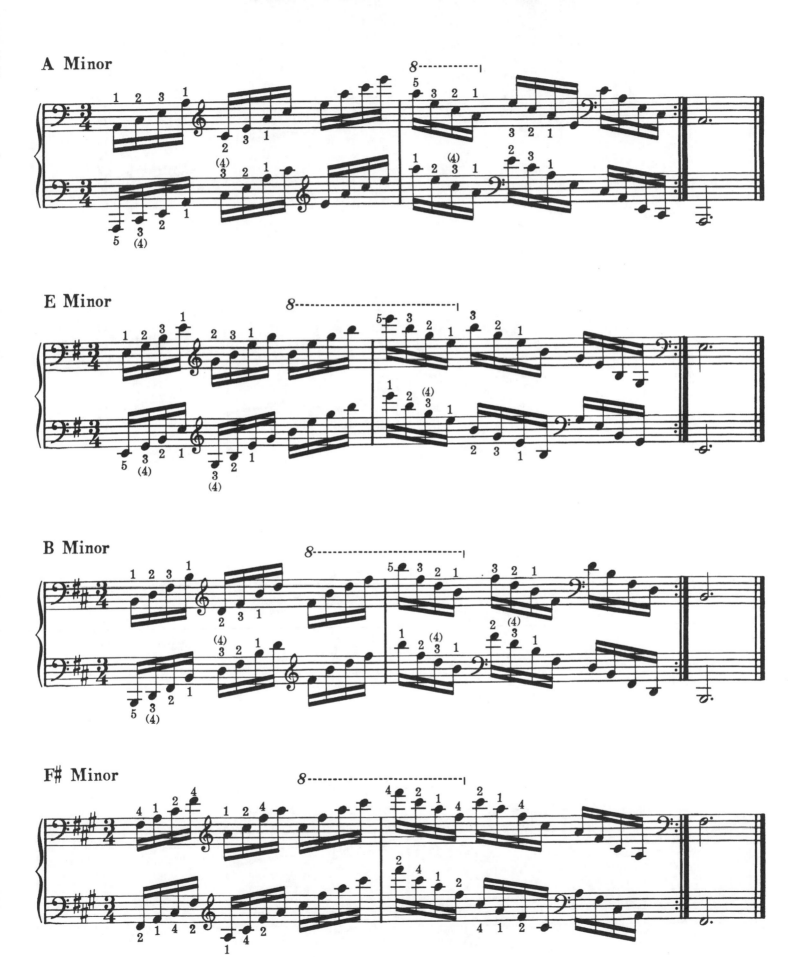

16. Minor Arpeggios of C♯, G♯, E♭, and B♭
(Four Octaves - Hands Together)

C# Minor

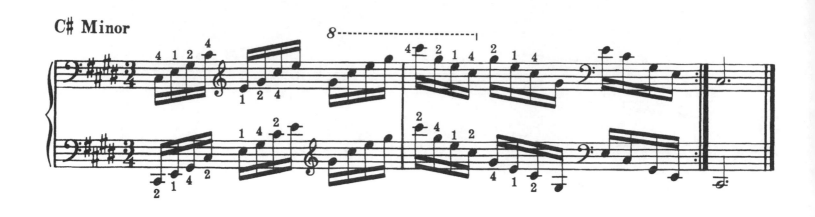

G# Minor

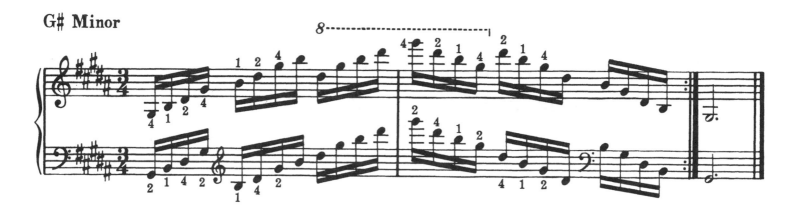

E♭ Minor

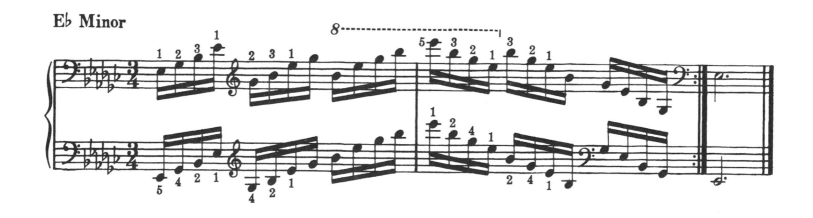

B♭ Minor

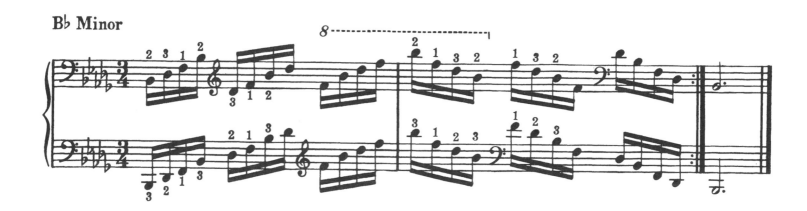

17. Minor Arpeggios of F, C, G, and D
(Four Octaves - Hands Together)

F Minor

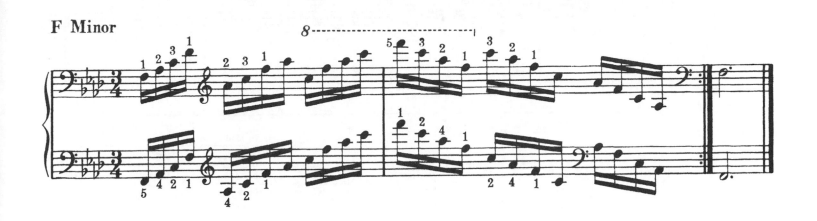

C Minor

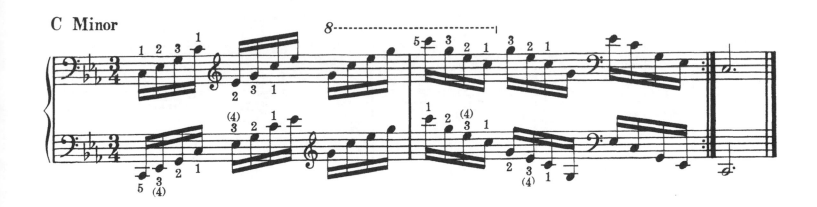

G Minor

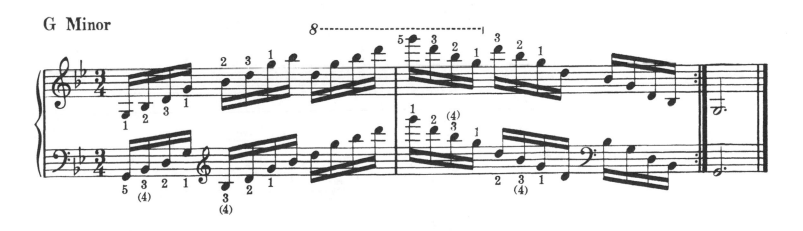

D Minor

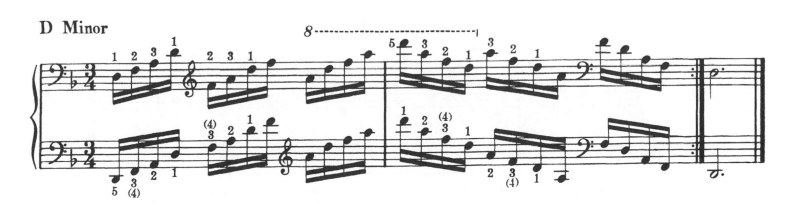

18. Minor Preludes in All Keys